VILLEFRANCE

Also by George Callaghan

Non Fiction
Artworks
George Callaghan Sketchbook
(How to be a Real Artist in 24 hours)

Childrens
100 Chocolate Soldiers
(Illustrated by George Callaghan)

callaghanprints.com
www.eakingallery.co.uk
www.gallerysalamanca.com.au
www.saddlerscourt.com

VILLEFRANCE

A French Mystery

by

GEORGE CALLAGHAN

with illustrations by

George Callaghan

ISBN: 978-1-4834-0896-5 (sc)
ISBN: 978-1-4834-0895-8 (e)

Library of Congress Control Number: 2014903275

Lulu Publishing Services rev. date: 03/03/2014

This novella is dedicated to my friend
Murcheen, Irish whistle and bodhran player
who lived life at one hundred miles an hour.

“We had Champagne that night
but real pain next morning
the night that we danced
at the Charladies Ball!”

CONTENTS

FOREWORD

I first met George in 1965 when we both joined a Sydney advertising agency as freelance Art Directors. It was obvious right from the start that he was a multi talented individual, not only developing advertising concepts but also designing packaging and even composing and singing the jingles. I can remember him breaking up an old piano and creating a dramatic piece of artwork using the wooden hammers. He made his own furniture without using nails or screws, the sections being held together with beautifully crafted wooden pegs, a very solid refectory table being one memorable piece. Not content with simply creating furniture he went on to build houses, one in Sydney featuring a complicated spiral staircase built around a large telegraph pole, and four other houses after he settled in Tasmania. George also turned his talents to making jewellery and fine art pieces in silver. One commission for the Bishop of Bendigo included a cross, ring and crosier.

As a gifted musician he could easily have pursued a career as a guitarist and singer, but it is his love affair with the harp that set George apart from most other musicians. Not content with learning to play the instrument he also decided to make and sell his own harps including unique harps made from carbon fibre, another from brass and leather and one from aluminium and horse hide.

His harp playing lead to numerous appearances on national and international television and radio. George has now recorded six c.d.'s.

George has regular exhibitions in Tasmania, England and Ireland most works being sold even before the opening night.

His landscapes are more than just landscapes, with his sense of design creating images that have an almost magical quality to them. When I look at one of his paintings I feel that all his other talents are evident in what he has created on the canvas. I can feel his skill as a musician, his Irish sense of humour, his craftsmanship all interwoven, giving the painting a quality that brings the most ordinary, everyday subjects to vibrant life.

His sculptures also have these qualities, the beauty seen by him in simple objects being transformed into unusual and unique creations.

This book is further proof of the creativity and vision of a truly multi talented artist.

Frank Palmer, Creative Director.

PREFACE

"All art is a poor reflection of reality" Perhaps the least creative member of the community is the artist, after all he is only acting as a mirror image of life.

In this novella you will encounter many characters chosen at random from my thousands of character sketches illuminated in my mind. They have been woven around a true incident. You yourself will have experienced many, many such characters.

Brenda's situation I have enjoyed many times before and this story could have been presented in any of my home towns in South Africa, Ireland, England, Tasmania, France.

Or anywhere in Australia after the election of Neville Bonner, the first Aborigine (real Australian) to be elected to parliament. Or when my good friend and photographer was refused membership of the Australian Returned Soldiers League (RSL).....he was a German returned soldier!

I have always kept a sketch book to record my daily observations. This novella is a short tiny glimpse at my notes.

Slainte!
George

ACKNOWLEDGMENTS

Thanks to my best friend ever for her
support, as only she knows how.

My editor Clare Winfield and George Shaw
of the Leprechauns fame.

INTRODUCTION

This novella started life as my next exhibition of paintings at the Eakin Gallery Belfast, a collection of portraits of characters from traditional folk songs. Instead of reaching for my paintbrush I reached for a pen. Any likeness to anyone is purely coincidental and unintentional.

Fifty year old Brenda, on the morning after her election to the council of the French village, Villefrance, discovers that the flowers and the planter boxes that she has personally paid for have been uprooted, overturned and strewn around the village square.

She assumes that it is the work of someone that she has upset within the hamlet of Villefrance.

The Mayor has gone on holiday and the Mairie is closed.

While waiting for the Mayor to return, she contemplates and makes a list of the people that she might have offended.

UPROOTED

Not only were all the plants totally uprooted, but the planter boxes had been upturned and were scattered around the entire village square.

"Who could have done such a horrible thing?" Had she been at home in England, she would have instantly blamed the local children, but No! This was France and children just didn't behave like that, especially in a country village. Brenda started turning over in her mind just who she had offended so badly. She knew that she had stepped on several toes to get herself onto the village council. Maybe she had ascended her position too rapidly.

She reflected on the last council meeting. Had it been her suggestion to personally pay for a series of planter boxes, complete with geraniums and Dutch tulips? And so soon after her election to the council?

The mayor and deputy mayor had seemed delighted with the idea. Still, she had a feeling of uneasiness, because this was the first appointment of a foreigner, let alone an English one to boot, to the council of Villefrance. Some of the outlying farms were engaged in feuds that went further back than Joan of Arc.

There was that recent incident when someone, a foreigner, had put flowers, lavender to be precise, on a shrine beyond the village boundaries. The culprit passed the shrine as usual on her way to the village shop, only to find the lavender strewn all over the road. She had not thought to offend anyone, since the date on the shrine went back long before the battle of Waterloo.

But no one in the village could object to Brenda's choice of beautiful flowers, though she wasn't absolutely sure of her choice of planter boxes. She had ended up with the pseudo concrete ones, rather than the traditional terra-cotta Greek/French urns. No! No! It couldn't be any of the villagers. None of them would complain about the boxes not being traditionally French, as 60 percent of the inhabitants were English, and the rest were Australian, Irish, South African, New Zealand, and Scottish. It was humorously claimed that within the boundaries of the village one could drive on the left-hand side of the road! The village might not exist if it had not been for the foreigners who restored most of the houses. The time might come when the entire village council would be made up of foreigners, and English would be spoken in preference to French.

Brenda sat down on a crumbling stone wall and considered having a bloody good cry, before putting all the plants back in their planter boxes. Already, there was a plan developing in her brain. Her husband had bought a motion-sensitive camera to help with their interest in wildlife. She decided she would mount it out of sight that night and see if she could catch the vengeful bastard.

In the meantime, “Well! We will hear what the mayor has to say about all of this!” Brenda stormed.

But even as Brenda approached the *mairie*, she remembered that the mayor was in Scotland on his annual fishing trip.

The deputy mayor would have to do, but then she recalled that the *mairie* offices only opened on Wednesdays! Get it right, thought Brenda; there are only so many hours in the week when the French are open for business, not including holidays. Mondays? Well, we don’t know whether we will open or not, but I think we should knock off for two or three hours for lunch and maybe we will open at 3:00 or 4:00. The public servants in the country are only open on Wednesdays, Thursdays, and Fridays, as long as the cafes and bars are shut! And everything shuts down on Sunday morning, unless there is an “R” in the month!

The Mayor fishing in Scotland

OAK LEAVES

Brenda seemed to be usually attired in half-finished garments. She seemed to favour unfinished crochet squares, preassembled in logarithm fashion. Her undergarments had a tendency to appear in a southerly direction, which gave her the appearance of a confused magpie. Although she definitely wore no frills, she seemed covered in them. Her features were many and assembled at random. She wore an expression of someone in a continual search of her lost crochet hook! Her shoes were much too broad, which caused her to be continually underfoot of herself.

She had headed the committee to obtain another oak leaf for the community. This was a series of ratings that gave status to the villages around France regarding their gardens and displays of flowers. It must be remembered that a committee designed the camel. Was this the same committee who had not only installed the village sundial on the North side of the *mairie* building (the shaded side!) but was also responsible for the newfangled hanging gardens of Babylon, again on the shaded side, and under cover, avoiding rain, and everything soon dying instantly for lack of sun and moisture?

On a committee of plant lovers, feelings ran deep. Brenda had, of course, supplied out of her own pocket, the planter boxes, complete with flowers. Surely, this exempted her of any further responsibility toward these flowers. There was no way she was going to bow down and water them! And No! She wasn't going to buy into the argument between *Mademoiselle* Bodica vs. *Madame* Azena.

Madame Azena was the self-appointed guardian of the church whose hairy head looked like a whirl of curly hair. On closer inspection, those curls turned out to be flies in constant motion. Her neck was surrounded by double chins, both back and front. One layer of chins was the result of a thyroid operation of the generous type.

She had a bosom as huge as watermelons, which she would hoist over her shoulders to fall with a thud on the dining table extinguishing all the candles that lived in fear of her presence. She was always out of breath but managing (just!) to keep in reserve enough oxygen for her perpetual cigars. Like all French ladies of distinction, she wore frills. In fact, even her frills had frills. But it was her shoes that won most of the attention from the casual observer. There weren't any!

How she managed to have sparks coming from her heels was a source of constant wonder!

Mademoiselle Bodica, keeper of the memorial square, on the other hand, was so diminutive that often she just wasn't there. At the times when she could be seen, everyone agreed that she always wore her underwear over her outer garments. There were times when she confused all concerned by wearing a dressing gown while out and about, leaving everyone in a heightened state of anticipation. Her hair was worn tight against her head, or perhaps she constantly wore a bathing hat with the intention or the possibility of going for a swim. Individually, her features were larger than her entire face.

She had been left at the altar, or had she altered the altar to make room for the resting place for the old cracked church bell?

In the meantime, no one seemed to notice that Bootie, the Afrikaner, had added an oak leaf of his own to the Villefrance signs outside the village boundaries. They were up there for several months before he removed them. Actually, he removed *all* the oak leaves, and still no one noticed!

Brenda felt she was now alone in the mission to see that the village would retain its one and only oak leaf.

If she had looked more carcfully, shc would have noticed that the village could be approached from four different directions. And each sign bore a different number of oak leaves.

Perhaps an Elm leaf?

FLIBBERTIGIBBET

Brenda decided that when she got home, with the help of her husband, Brian, she would make a list of all the people she might possibly have upset. Surely, this would be easy, as there could not be many who Brenda had offended. Three or four at most—perhaps five!

With each step she travelled home, she realized she was adding to her list. At this rate, the list would be endless by the time she got home. Being a POM (prisoners of her majesty) as the Aussies called her, perhaps she would handle it like an Agatha Christie mystery. However, this did not suit Brenda's flibbertigibbet brain. Twenty-four hours later, she was still adding to her list of suspects. She was all over the place with her plans, and her suspicions changed willy-nilly every two minutes.

Brian had listened with sympathy to her sad dilemma. On his considered advice, she paused to digest all of his ideas.

He had said, "Sit down, catch your breath, and remember you are British, from military stock! Do as your ancestors would have done, make yourself a military plan of attack, work out your boundaries, objectives, blah, blah, blah!"

Sometimes, he really annoyed her with his ramblings. Here she was, her world in turmoil, and he was going off on one of his soliloquies!

"No! I will stick to my usual beating-about-the-bush strategy," concluded Brenda.

Already, her list was all over the place and as long as her list of birthdays:

Madame Azena
Belle-De-Jour
Bluey the Aussie

Bootie
Madame Bodica
Liam
Richard
Maris
Mick
La Patrimoine
Percer
Seamus etc, etc, etc.....

She had been at her list, beautifully written and in alphabetical order, for quite some time when the horrible thought struck her. If so many people had a beef with her, and she had so many problems with so many people, what *was* she doing in France, anyway?

How to listen sympathetically.

THE WEATHER

Brenda and Brian had made their fortune back home importing exotic timbers from the Antipodeans into the European and UK markets. Like all Brits, their success was measured in the length of their swimming pool. But, Brenda had often wondered what the point was of having a swimming pool when you fall victim to every Englishman's dilemma—THE WEATHER!

She could have chosen to live in Spain, Italy, or Portugal, but she had schoolgirl French, and it was as simple as that.

There were many things she enjoyed about France. The weather. The health system. The politics. The fact that all French politicians came pre-bribed made them unbribeable, and you couldn't blackmail a politician either, not when he was being blackmailed already. She rather enjoyed the fact that mistresses could be claimed legitimate expenses, too.

She had thought that she loved French food, but that had waned after two months of eating from all the restaurants, all cooking from the same menu, in a 500 kilometre radius! But she certainly loved the grog. She had been perpetually sozzled since her arrival in 1990!

Of course, there were fewer cars on the road, and it sounded exotic when she phoned home and told her friends that she drove a Peugeot with proper pronunciation, or when she told of Brian's Renault with a silent "t."

Nowadays, shc was so chuffed to have made it onto the local council. It never crossed her mind that she might have bribed herself onto the committee with her generous donations to the council's slush fund.

Is this a legitimate tax deduction?

VILLEFRANCE

Villefrance had seen better days. There were days in winter when it saw no days at all.

The village had seen several changes of street lighting, from oil, gas, and now electricity. Then, the streets were uprooted to install the sewer and again, to install broadband.

There was a cafe lost in one corner of the shadows in the village square. Above, towered the church spire, which cast perpetual intimidation across the village. Its bells chimed the hour every ten minutes, twice on weekdays and reluctantly on public holidays. The architecture belonged to the *Patrimoine*, but the contents still belonged to Rome, however, bad taste and bad aesthetics were influenced by its historic charm. The priest was of the understanding that he owned the place, even though no one ever attended it, except for an unanticipated death. The rest of the square was surrounded by *boulangeries* and pharmacies with green-flashing signs; the restaurant advertised the inevitable *Canard De Foie Gras*, among terrified *Pommes de la Nuit*.

The village was on the side of a hill and contained a collection of unusable stone steps in the upward direction. There was one flight that came down, but this was under repair. The village cemetery was elevated above ground; the retaining walls oozing ghosts. On All Saints Eve, layer upon layer of chrysanthemums were laid on the graves to contain the underworld.

The current pride of the town was the new bell. The sundial on the shaded side of the square replaced a fountain that had run afoul of a rampant bus.

The village had its weekly market, where shoppers were charged twice as much as the nearest supermarket, and where they allowed you to touch the goods. Then there was the monthly *vide-grenier*, where everyone was diddled for a clinking, clanking collection of collagenous assorted junk from the Land of Oz.

The *mairie* was of the elevated variety and was adorned with numerous shutters, which the previous *mairie* had painted an unpopular shade of maroon. It was a choice of colour that had caused him to lose the last election. The incumbent *mairie* had been currently misplaced.

The village had had its heyday when a larger than normal carp was caught in a nearby lake. All agreed that the village was now in decline due to the size of its *boule* players.

Not the size of the carp surely?

THE BELL

Of course, everyone knew of the fiasco with the bell, so there was an endless list of those who would have it in for Brenda.

What had started with a slip of the tongue had ended in a unanimous acceptance of her proposal. Over this issue, the entire community had it in for her. She was the little boy who had exposed the pretence of the Emperor's invisible clothes.

At the town council meeting relating to the commissioning of a new church bell (the old one having cracked 200 years ago), someone suggested that the bell should carry on one side an image of Christ, and that perhaps, as this was a farming community, he should be surrounded by cows. This went down a treat, until someone pointed out that this was goat-cheese country. All agreed that goats it should be! What about geese? No! Not geese! We don't produce *foie gras*!

"Ah," someone pointed out, "didn't Christ have something to do with sheep?"

Yes, that was it! They would show Christ among a flock of sheep with a forked stick in his hand (the parable and the image of Christ with the lost lamb tucked under his arm, holding a shepherd's crook, was lost on the evening breeze coming through an open window).

So now the south side of the bell had an image of Christ among some strange animals. The east side of the bell had an image of St. Luke, the patron Saint of Scribes. But that seemed strange, because the village was not renowned for any culture, least of all its authors. But the west side of the bell was to be a tribute to the oldest patron of the church in the village. That left the north side vacant.

This was where Brenda dropped her clanger.

"I know," said Brenda. "Since there are now more English people living here than French, why not use the image of St. George and the dragon?"

There it was; she had blurted it out! Everyone agreed that this suggestion was a splendid one!

The meeting had turned rather amicable, and no one, up to this point, had taken offence at Brenda's suggestion. It was that know-it-all bastard, Bootie, who threw the Spaniard into the works! Just at the time when the mould had been cast for the bell, and they were about to pour the final casting, he pointed out to the council committee that the actual church had been dedicated to Saint Michael, who, in the Book of Revelation, battled with and slew Satan. St. Michael was represented outside their church slaying Satan, who had human features with wings and a tail; he was NOT a Dragon!

There was thousands of euros invested in this project. The government had supplied a grant for half the funding, and the community was expected to pay the balance. Yes, Brenda had made a lot of enemies that day explaining to the committee that their patron saint, Saint Michael and the devil, had been usurped by England's St. George and a fire-breathing dragon.

When the bell was finally unveiled, everyone wanted to know if St. Michael was the one slaying a fire-breathing dragon?

It would have been easy enough to change the legend in the mould below the image of St. George to read St. Michael.

Yes, a clanger had certainly been dropped that day.

I'm a patron saint.

MARIS

Maris, the music teacher, had a lot to answer for. Brenda agreed with the old saying, "Those who can, do; those who can't, teach!" That music teacher was a nasty kettle of fish! She had the attitude of a Valhalla Bride and a Valkyries widow. Her gown had been made from concert hall curtains complete with curtain hooks. She never bothered cutting the sash cord to length. Instead, she wrapped it three times around her ample midriff.

Brenda claimed that her son had perfect pitch, or was it pitch perfect? Whatever! Brenda was very proud of him.

"Oh, I am terribly sorry to hear that," had been Maris's retort.

Brenda ignored her reply, thinking that she had misheard her, but later, after a consultation with her husband, she decided to confront Maris.

"Did I hear you right when you offered your sympathies when I told you that my son had pitch perfect?"

"Yes, you did," replied Maris.

"But why?"

"Simple," explained Maris. "It means that there is too much music that he can't enjoy."

"Come off it!" exclaimed Brenda.

"No," replied Maris, "you have made a classic and easy mistake. The fact that your son is pitch perfect is not something to boast about. At its best, anyone who is pitch perfect can give a starting point for an ensemble of musicians. From there on, it is all downhill. If someone is out of tune, it is intolerable. If the music has been transposed to a different key, it is unbearable, and if the music is out of concert pitch, well...say no more."

This was a revelation, and it didn't sit well with Brenda. But there were other reasons she didn't like music teachers. Twice she had had encounters with them. The first time was when her oldest daughter was rejected by the school choir. She had stormed into the principal's office demanding to see the music teacher. What did she mean that her daughter wasn't good enough for the school choir? Wasn't the whole purpose of schooling, surely, to teach those who couldn't sing, to sing?

The second encounter was with another school teacher. Her younger daughter was selected for the school choir and was told what an honour this was. When the younger daughter enquired as to what songs they would be singing, she declined joining the choir on the grounds that she wasn't prepared to sing any of that old rubbish! Brenda insisted again that the choir was there to exalt the school and was made up of those who could sing, denying tuition to those who couldn't sing.

Brenda thought of Pedro, her closest male friend. He had just discovered that he was a beautiful singer. He loved music and had spent his early life humming and trying to remember tunes to play on the piano and harp that were on loan from a friend. But he had worked all his life as a stone mason, and now, the muscles in his arms and hands were muscle-bound. His tendons gave up in disgust. However, he discovered that he could sing! No one quite knew how this was realized, but he finally decided to take singing lessons.

"What a fantastic voice," exclaimed the teacher! "First thing we will have to do is get rid of those dreadful French vowels, pronounced from the highest level of your nasal passage. The vowels must be pronounced softly as in Italian...I'm Italian," exclaimed the teacher proudly. "Edith Piaf and Charles Aznavour were enough for the French. They're over it, and they are in the past!"

When Pedro related this story to Brenda, she replied, "But even the French hate their own music now. Have you noticed there are no French recordings of singers being played in public places? In shops and supermarkets, they are singing in American or English."

But yes, Brenda had plenty of experience of the folly of music teachers. And she was convinced Maris could tell!

Maris in one of her moods.

THE AUSSIE

What was it that the smart arse Australian musician had said to her when she sang the praises of the singer who performed at the local cafe? What was it he said? Hmmm. Oh yes, there are 60,000 singers in France, and they are all called Charles Aznavour! Smart little tyrant!

In real Aussie language, Bluey was built like a brick shithouse door. His shoulders were the width of the Sydney Harbour Bridge, his features were akin to the opera house, and gave him the appearance of a freshly hatched chook. It was said that he had a heart as big as Ayers Rock. He was called Bluey, after Bluey Brink from the Australian song he was always singing.

Now there once was a shearer, by the name Bluey Brink,
A devil for work and a devil for drink.
He could shear his two hundred each day without fear,
He could drink without winking four gallons of beer.

Now Jimmy, the barman, who served out the drink,
He hated the sight of this here Bluey Brink.
Who stayed much too late and who came much too soon
At evening, at morning, at night and at noon.

One morning as Jimmy was cleaning the bar
With sulphuric acid he kept in a jar,
Old Bluey came yelling and bawling with thirst,
"Whatever you got, Jim, just hand me the first."

Now, it ain't in the history, it ain't put in print,
But Bluey drank acid with never a wink,
Saying, "That's the stuff, Jimmy, why, strike me stone
dead.
This'll make me the ringer of Stevenson's shed."

Now all that long day, as he served out the beer,
Poor Jimmy was sick with his trouble and fear.
Too worried to argue, too anxious to fight,
Seeing the shearer a corpse in his fright.

But the next day while Jimmy was opening the bar,
Along came the shearer craving for more;
With his eyebrows all singed and his whiskers deranged,
And holes in his hide like a dog with the mange.

"Well," says Jimmy to Bluey, "And how's the new stuff?"
Said Bluey, "It was fine, but I ain't had enough.
For it gives me great courage to shear and to fight,
But why does this stuff set my whiskers alight?

I thought I knew drink but I must have been wrong,
For what you just give me was proper and strong.
It set me to coughing, and you know I'm no liar
And every cough sets my whiskers on fire."

Brenda and Bluey hadn't hit it off since his arrival in the village. He had spent a couple of years in her homeland, England, before coming to France and had no appreciation for the social graces observed in her country.

What was all that cow tailing and forelock doffing to certain levels of society and calling people sir? The Aussie just didn't get it.

He understood that a certain amount of *this sir, and that sir* had existed in Oz, but all that had died with Captain Cook.

The Aussie mongrel just didn't understand how important it was for society to maintain the standards of support for bad music, bad theatre, and bad food. All these bad issues were to be supported as examples of how bad things could really get.

For example, Brenda was proud of the fact that she was totally tone deaf. She was of a mind to support all music, although she liked to be seen to patronise what she thought was classical. This was easy to define as there are only two kinds of music in France—classical and jazz. That Aussie lout insisted that there was much more and had muttered something about blues, folk, soul, rock, country, reggae, etc.

Brenda and Bluey hitting it off.

BLUEY AND KIWI

Bluey and Kiwi were always at each other's throats, and most of their frustrations with each other were vented in the local cafe. As an Australian, Bluey was of the opinion that all Kiwis were at heart Welsh farmers, each having a personal relationship with their favourite sheep.

Bluey was still thriving on his one-upmanship that he had won over the Kiwis in their last row. Of all things to barney over, this one was fly spray!

"Sure the stuff they use here in France actually attracts flies! I have seen a wasp's nest built between two cans of French insect repellent. Down under, we have stuff that repels sharks!"

And so it went on until Bluey struck a blow beneath the belt, introducing the British Monarch into the argument.

"Back in '62 when her majesty," (spoken in terms of reverence), "made her first visit to God's own country, the CSIRO, the government scientific body developed a fly repellent for her to use. But at the last moment, the officials were too inhibited to use it on her actual ladyship. In the entourage, she was the only one without it on, and every fly from miles around descended on her. There wasn't any TV footage or a newspaper photo where she wasn't surrounded by flies! The next day, she was saturated with the fly repellent and not a fly accosted her!"

Then Bluey added with fire, "Her ladyship's next port of call was your leach-ridden ditch, ya mongrel! You Kiwis asked for a ton of the stuff to be shipped in time for her majesty's visit!"

Brenda knew that the moment the queen was mentioned, it was time to move on. So, she never knew the result of that debate/ punch up!

It is a great way to catch flies.

BELLE DE JOUR

Brenda was remembering that horrible day she had spent having her beauty treatment. The day started with having her inner soul cleansed and beautified with an hour-long session of yoga.

"Om Padme ooom," had resounded in her head. Having vowed never to join in any of this religious chanting rubbish, she had looked at her friend seated beside her who was grinning in apparent bliss with her eyes closed.

Intriguingly, the yoga exercises promised to improve Brenda's repertoire of sexual positions, if only she could get her husband to join in!

Belle-de-jour, the beautician, had looked up the meaning of *beautiful* in the dictionary, and she decided that this was definitely her. She was beautiful in every direction; every feature she had added to with abundance. She moon-bathed in the nude to avoid bra and knicker shadows. Her fashion sense had been learnt from her mother who was a pyro-technician.

While her feet were meaningless, her inverted bosom attracted the strangest of associates. She was a walking cosmetician, coffier, podiatrist, and mistress of any other beauty treatment she could cash in on. Her platinum bleached hair arrived hours before she did, while her fingernails beat an endless tattoo on her crammed plastic vanity case.

When she arrived, she was a haze of patchouli oil and she left with contrails of currency. Perhaps she had a sexy husky voice, but this was lost at the end of a cigar holder that hung from her watery, limp hand.

Then it was time for the internal anal probe, or was it called *colonic irrigation*? Did that mean swallowing some kind of towel and extruding it from the other end? Hmmm. Perhaps this was the reason for the menial lunch. Then her imagination ran wild.

Well,Brenda thought later, that hadn't been as bad as she had supposed! But what was meant by the removal of all those toxins?

This incident she added to her lengthening list of alternative medical crap. She recalled how her husband had attended an iridologist out of curiosity. What was the problem? Brian claimed he had high blood pressure.

"Let's examine your eyes then! Hmm, well, your liver's shot. Your kidneys are hardly functioning, and it won't be long before diabetes kicks in! Let's check your blood pressure. My god, you are nearly off the scale!"

"Of course it is nearly off the scale! You've just told me my liver is shot, my kidneys don't function, and I have diabetes! Whose blood pressure wouldn't rise after that diagnosis?"

The inner soul had been fine-tuned, and the inner self had been irrigated. Now it was time for the beauty treatment.

Brenda prided herself on her natural beauty and unblemished complexion. She reclined and closed her eyes, hoping to drift off, while her nails and hands were attended to. Lotion was smoothed over her entire face and light stone pebble weights were applied to her cheeks, chin, and forehead. After a while, there was a slight burning sensation, which she was assured was quite normal. Again, it was those toxins coming out. The sensation lingered, and she began to worry. Sure enough, when the weights were removed from her face and Belle-de-jour the beautician began to remove the face lotion, a look of horror spread over her face.

"What, what, what?" Brenda hollered as the beautician fled in search of cold water.

Brenda sat bolt upright and searched for the mirror. Her entire face had turned raw red from ear to ear. The yoga group was thrown into a panic as every home-grown remedy was tried, but to no avail! The burning seemed to go on for hours, and Brenda was coping with the possibility of being scarred for life.

Belle-de-jour, the beautician, was defending her treatment by demonstrating how the products she used were all natural.

"Look! All the boxes have flowers on them! Why, the one I used on Brenda's face had roses on it!"

When Brenda's skin had finally calmed enough for her to walk home covered in cucumbers, she had to pay full whack for the day's beauty treatment!

There were others who talked of the incident. Brenda never mentioned it herself, but the news was on the bush telegraph. The beauty parlor became a faded memory. Was Brenda to blame for its demise? Was Belle-de-jour to be added to her growing list of suspects?

Gathering beauty pebbles.

ARCHERY

Brenda realized as she plodded her weary, wayward home that she had started making enemies from the moment she had arrived in France twelve years ago. She had vowed not to fall into the trap and become what Bluey the Aussie would call, "Another bloody whinging Pom!" But, no sooner had she committed to this idea, than she had put her foot in it, in one of the worst ways possible.

Her husband, Brian, was a keen archer, and he had won numerous medals in competitions held throughout the UK. Nothing grand like a position of first, second, or third in the national championships and not even in the top ten. Brenda kidded him that most of his medals were awarded just for showing up, as there seemed to be medals awarded for everything, even for wearing the most successful camouflage gear of the shoot. If only they could find someone to award it to!

During their first months in France, Brian had located the local field archery club in their department. As luck would have it, the club was holding their national championships, and Brian was encouraged to compete as he had all his documentation from the NFS in England, which proved that he was aware of all the safety rules of the sport (not that safety was an issue with the French archers).

Brian accompanied himself during rounds of archery with his beautiful tenor singing voice, which he claimed he had inherited from Allan-a-Dale. His broad shoulders came from Little John, his firm deep chest belonged to Much-The-Miller and his dress sense he defiantly inherited from Will Scarlet. All in all, he wouldn't blame anyone for mistaking him for Robin Hood! In reality, he looked like Woody Allen in drag.

Brenda was always there to support Brian in these events, and it was promising to be a good day. Brian seemed to be holding his own among his fellow competitors. He even managed a round of applause when he got a hit on the target of the Duke of Wellington!

They had completed the morning round of the course when lunch break was announced. Brenda retired to their vehicle to collect the packed lunch of ham and pickle and a flask of good old Rosie Lee.

When she returned to the meeting place, it was deserted except for Brian whose French at this time was almost nil. He explained that he thought they were to follow down a particular track and join the others at a picnic area. They travelled down the track some fifty meters, until they reached a clearing in the woods with a huge ramshackle shed. Inside, it was lined with trestle tables and benches. Smoke was billowing from an open spit and the smell of gold was on the air. A roast pig was rotating on a spit with one of those wind-up things that you buy at *Vide Greniers* throughout France, and there was a line of archers waiting for their potion of Pork.

"*Rejoindre la file d'attente*!" was the command from Jacques the club secretary, gesturing towards a disorderly queue.

"But, but, we bought our own sandwiches."

But an explanation was wasted among the merry men and women.

There followed two hours of French hospitality—*foie gras* for starters, pork, *pommes frites*, string beans, carrots, then the cheeses of which there were Heinz 57 varieties, followed by *creme brulee*. All the food was washed down by copious amounts of red wine. The two-hour luncheon was rounded off with a special 500 proof cider, specially brewed for the occasion!

Now for the second round of archery.

At the day's end, the usual medals were awarded for all the different sections: bare bow, compound bow, long bow, women's section, etc. Then camc thc *coup de grâcc*! The highest score of the day—Brenda's Brian!

What had started as an orderly game of archery before lunch had ended as a drunken traipsing around the countryside, in the words of Fred Wedlock's song, "firing arrows here and there," at anything that resembled a target. There was a stage where arrows were fired willy-nilly above the horizon. Brenda and Brian almost headed for home, when someone started firing arrows directly into the air overhead.

Of course, Brian won this award for the highest score! He wasn't drunk! He didn't drink!

During the coming week, Brenda retold the story to anyone who would listen. Looking back now, she reflected that she should have not concluded her story with, "No wonder the French lost at Agincourt!" She thought that at the time she meant this as a compliment; the French had much better things to do than fight a war! Like food, drink, and sex, in that order. But now she knew to never mention Agincourt!

Brian said it was music.

THE PATRIMOINE

Brenda was starting to get paranoid. Surely not everyone had it in for her. She would get to the root of this mischief and put all this paranoia behind her. She would never let the paranoia get hold of her like it did her friend Cynthia's husband who stopped following rugby, because every time there was scrum, he was of the mind that both teams were talking about him.

Now, who was next on her list? In this instance, several, and they were all on the tip of her tongue—yes, the *Patrimoine*. This was a group of progressive or regressive people who allocated funding for the maintenance of historical buildings within the community. This included private dwellings. Brenda had referred to them in an open conversation as a bunch of self-serving, self-satisfying megalomaniacs with parasols.

As with all services in France, everything is bound up in red tape, but the French were used to the tape, and they had the patience of Job. Each of these services refused admission unless you could produce the necessary green form, which was available only from the establishment that you were trying to enter. One of the major provisos of obtaining a grant to improve your historic home was that on a specific day of the year (*les journees du Patrimoine*), your home would be open to the public.

Of course, this was open to massive abuse. In fact, whole industries were based on this.

The day of the *Patrimoine* was upon the village. The fashion shops, the cosmetic departments, and the coiffeurs in the nearest towns had done a roaring trade, selling what in polite terms could only be called disguises. This was everyone's opportunity to find out just what their neighbours were spending their money on. What new furniture had they bought? Was it carpets, curtains, or food in the kitchen cupboards? It was open season on privacy.

This seemed to Brenda to be at odds with the French, whom she thought were rather a private lot. Hadn't she read that the shutters on the public side of the homes in France were kept closed since the French Revolution in 1789? That was done in case they were dobbed in (as the French are inclined to do) to *Monsieur Guillotine* as possibly a wealthy aristocrat. Brenda also knew that you could be talking to a French person you had just met for hours, and they would never tell you their name.

Standing at the bar of the village cafe in the midst of a group dressed in their finest refinery, Brenda tried to bite her tongue, but went on to say what everyone knew, "Aren't we all just a bunch of nosey parkers?"

She could only hope that her outburst had gone unnoticed, perhaps distracted by Bluey the Australian's claim that back in Oz they had a similar way of invading a person's privacy.

"Struth! Any old bastard can come on your property and fish in your dam or lakes if the fisheries have seeded it! Back home in my state of Tasmania, there are no natural native salmon or trout in our rivers or lakes. The inland fisheries breed them at a place called Salmon Ponds about 30ks from Hobart. The young are released into the rivers, and when they mature, if they are not caught, they make their way back to where their ancestors came from. The fisheries will stock any dam or lake on your private property with the same proviso as that of the *Patrimoine*. Any member of the public is allowed to trespass and fish in any dam or lake that has been seeded by the fisheries department."

Like those panoramic photographs of the resistance fighters on display in the *Mussee de la Resistance*, which gave the Nazi's an identikit of all the egotists in town, the *Patrimoine* were too busy jostling for a position in the line-up for the annual photograph to take any notice of Brenda or Bluey's comments.

We've gotta get our guns into the picture!

ANTON LAURENT LAVOISIER

When Brenda spelled out the word as Psycho-the-rapist, it didn't amuse Anton at all! Again, she was putting her tuppence-worth in on the conversation and stamping her authority over the newcomer, getting his back up immediately.

She continued, "Isn't psychotherapy a profession where someone is paying you to be their friend?"

She didn't say she thought that all psychotherapists needed psychotherapy themselves. That is how they were actually dragged into the profession. She had a few friends back in England who attended psychotherapists, so she felt she was on safe ground in giving her opinion. It was costing them a fortune, week after week, as they became more and more dependent on their psychotherapist to make it through the day, unable to make a decision for themselves. Surely, it was in Anton's interest NOT to help his clients. Surely, each client cured would diminish his income.

Brenda loved to quote her husband, Brian. He was an authority on everything and wasn't into new-age therapy, aromatherapy, crystals, Reiki healing and the old age therapy of acupuncture.

Brian had read somewhere that in Britain, unless you were a registered practitioner of medicine, it was against the law to break the skin of anyone. All acupuncturists and tattoo artists were acting outside of the law!

Then, there were chiropractors. When the patient felt and heard his bones crack, he thought that he was instantly cured. It was a trick every child could do when they cracked their knuckles. And what about the chiropractor's main answer to his patients' problems?

"No wonder you are in such a bad way! Look! One leg is shorter than the other. For that we will have to x-ray you—60 euros immediately. Now, look, see? One leg is shorter than the other, just as I expected. Your hips have to compensate with a lean in one direction, then your shoulders have to re-compensate in the opposite direction, which constantly tilts your head. No wonder you get those headaches! As for your spine, it is all over the place! We will have to adjust that C1."

(Half the hippies in the seventies had their C1 adjusted twice a week, which instantly readjusted itself at the first sound of an alarming car horn!)

"Not to worry! We will have that all realigned in ten visits!"

"Bullshit!" said Brenda's husband. "Everyone has one leg shorter than the other. It's nature's way of ensuring we never wander far from home, and we always wander in ever decreasing circles."

Like all psychotherapists, Anton was gullible to any new-fangled idea that would offer a shortcut to their goals—pills, snake oil medicines, contraptions, and workshop junkies. Brenda looked at Anton sceptically. He should have been dressed in an ancient wizard's gown, definitely purple, adorned with crescent moons, stars, and zodiac signs. A wizard's pointy hat and wand would have completed his attire, but instead, he had the appearance of someone who had just stepped off the iceberg that had encountered the Titanic. His skin was sallow, and his features were devoid of all interest. His eyes were too close together and at times merged into one, which he thought was very cosmic. The fuzz on his face never really qualified as a beard. He had hands most people would have thought of as those of a musician which, in reality, were forever getting in the way when he tried to learn an instrument. His dress sense was boring, boring, boring! He wore a hat that was out of fashion even when hats were out of fashion. In fact, he was forever arriving too soon and leaving much too late. Didn't Bertrand from Bertrand's Circus claim there was a sucker born every minute?

Brenda thought she had gone too far when she exclaimed to Anton, "Isn't psychotherapy just another substitute for religion?"

Antons happy clients.

BOOTIE

Brenda felt pity for Iris. Why should this arrogant Boer of an Afrikaner pick on her? After all, she was just one more watercolour artist exhibiting at the village art gallery. There had been eight exhibitions during the summer, five of which were from painters. So, why pick on Iris?

"Because every year, it's the same here and at all the surrounding villages. Another bloody retiree who has come to France, puts on an exhibition, and feels that they can now call themselves an 'artist!' You are NOT an artist! It's like calling yourself, 'sir!' When others start calling you an artist, perhaps then and only then, you can call yourself an artist."

Brenda defended Iris by claiming that we are all artists. Bootie finally yielded.

"Yes, true, at this level, we are all artists."

Bootie was always ruffling someone's feathers. He had tried to give a series of lectures on art. Brenda tried to remember the list of ten lectures: Art is easy if you don't know what you are doing; Art must present not represent; Art is the pursuit of that which is not essential; All art is useless.

Surely, there was enough here to stimulate the community through the winter months, but the heated arguments after the third lesson made the continuance of the lectures impossible! After that, Bootie had to stop trying to explain just what art is, and he came to a conclusion that no one really knew just what it was, and in reality, therefore, art could not be taught.

Bootie had paintbrushes and tubes of oil paint that spread out of his four corners. This confused many art critics, since most of them considered the more art materials, the worse the artist. But Bootie was good. Nay, he was brilliant. His head was free of hair;

he maintained that his hair was long on the inside. His eyebrows had been sanded off, and his ears were automaton, huge, of which he had two. His nose had blood veins that had more in sympathy with a scouring pad, and his head was always adorned with an oil paint, stained handkerchief knotted at the four corners in English seaside fashion. He always wore his T-shirt and pullover inside out, declaring that if he should ever encounter the president of France, he'd have a fresh, clean ensemble of clothing on the inside ready for the occasion.

Brenda knew that for all Bootie's pedantic ways, what he said was true. He had come to the village from Cape Town, South Africa. He had studied at the Art College there for four years and later attended a further two years at the Slade School of Art in London. He had spent his life exhibiting around the world including Paris, New York, Sydney, and London.

Brenda had overheard numerous times when he was introduced to the latest member of the watercolour club set. As a famous, accomplished artist, it must have irked him somewhat to hear the instant unconsidered reply, "How exciting! I'm an artist too!"

"Do you know," Bootie once said, "that at the last count, there were just ten artists in England making their living from their art? That does not include teachers; I mean purely from making and selling their work. All other artists have a second job, which helps to support their work, or a patron, like a rich husband or a rich wife. This helps to undermine the value of not only their art, but all art, because they are able to undersell any artists like myself who are trying to support themselves. For instance, take any painting here! How long has it taken, including all the mistakes? How much money for paints, canvas, brushes, the mounts, and the framing? And what is the cost of the painting? One hundred and fifty euro at the most! One of my frames costs twice that. It can't be done unless someone pays for all this, especially for those that don't sell, bearing in mind that they will only sell to half a dozen intimidated friends, a rich aunt, someone they are trying to lay, a moron who will buy anything, and one exhibition only at that, never to be repeated. And then comes pottery, like the exhibition before this one. It was a complete sell-out!

Twenty pieces at 120 euro each! That is 2,400 euro. Wouldn't even pay for the kiln, let alone the electricity bill! Wouldn't keep me in cigars! And you ask, why pick on Iris? I'm fed up with being invited to yet another exhibition by the blue rinse set that call themselves artists! Or by another pseudo, nouveau artist who exhibits their first year's experiments, or by an artist whose work does not present but represents!"

"Then why come to the exhibition at all?" asked Brenda.

"I have come," replied Bootie, "to advise you all that I am doing what all retired Brits do. I am retiring from art to become an accountant."

Brenda had put Bootie on the spot. Was he out for revenge?

He's retiring you know to become an accountant.

THE PERCER

At dusk and the approach of eve, when the street lamps are coming on, a shuffling of feet can be heard through the village. You will probably be just in time to run to your window to catch a glimpse of a ghostly figure. If you are patient enough, the figure will eventually pass your window. The villagers refer to this apparition as the "Percer."

Two illuminated, spiral-shaped eyes stared from the shadow cast over his forehead by the enormous beret that was the entire width of his massive shoulders. His back was stooped from the entire weight of the world upon it.

He continually wobbled on his three legs, one of which was a very crooked walking stick, which he had found upon a very crooked style. His trousers and legs followed at a discreet distance. Most of his persona was dictated by his companion that was hard to identify, since it never stood still long enough for anyone to make a positive recognition. Whatever it was, he called it, *Vous*!

This figure used to only make its appearance in the absolute darkness of night, but as time went by, it started emerging through the mist of the day, in the company of that mangy, shaking, four-legged companion.

Nowadays, the phantom made its appearance in broad daylight, specifically on a Saturday, when the mobile shop made its visit to the village.

Brenda would occasionally see Percer when she visited the mobile shop for the groceries that she had failed to purchase in the nearby town. Perhaps Percer was responsible for the carnage. He had been reported to the mayor for smashing someone's garden gnomes, but "No," thought Brenda, Percer was surely harmless.

Up to the time when he had received his injury during a *Sanglier* shoot, *Monsieur* Jambon was just one of the lads. In French hunting fashion, he had idly stood around at the bottom of the track that had emerged from a wooded area with his comrades, smoking *Gauloises* and knocking back the red wine, when it emerged from the thicket area. Not even a grunt, it headed straight for him. His friends fled in all directions, dropping their guns as they ran. The boar trapped him between the double trunks of a forked tree as it proceeded to deprive him of his wedding tackle. The dogs appeared from down the track, and the pig took off. His drinking and smoking friends never did return and are still running. He was found later when the hunters went in search of their dogs.

Monsieur Jambon, for that was his name, regained consciousness in the hospital, minus his family jewels. From then on, he was constantly harassed by the local children, who chanted "*Qui a perdu ses testicules alors*?" ("Who has lost his testicles?")

Eventually, he became a recluse and was only to be seen painfully limping through the village when the children were soundly asleep in their beds. That was years ago, and because the children had all grown up, the teasing stopped. Now, he could be seen during daylight in the village.

"No," thought Brenda. It was not *Monsieur* Jambon. He was too much of a gentle man.

But Brenda remembered there was something else she had remarked about hunters. Yes, she recalled the remark she had foolishly made.

"French hunters behave like the Keystone Cops in search of Charlie Chaplin!"

Not that the French would know who either of these parties were. They stood in groups of ten or so at the end of a country track. At the sound of a horn, or the jingling of bells from the approaching dogs, with back up telephones, iPads, a GPS, and Google Earth, they would all hop into their four-wheel drives. In groups of two or three, they disappeared up the track only to re-emerge at the other end and rendezvous with another group of ten more equally confused hunters.

Yes, she was rather pleased with her comparison.

No, no, not the family jewels...

THE KIWI

There were also official reasons that had to be taken into consideration. One can't serve on the council without cracking eggs.

When a newcomer from New Zealand had to confront the mayor on an issue that he was spitting nails about, Brenda had been called in to act as an interpreter, because the Kiwi could only speak antipodean English. Of course, Brenda, being the messenger, would cop it from both sides.

The Kiwi's hair was of the traditional Maori style. It was long, white, and looked like a cloud. His face had a complexion that had started life as a tribal tattoo, but having a sensible aversion to pain, he had chickened out halfway through the process. His nose had more holes than necessary, but these days, he refused to wear his traditional piercing. He constantly sang American country songs, which he accompanied himself on a *woomera* he had borrowed from an Aussie. Around his ankles, he sprayed shark and snake repellent that really worked. He was never bothered by them.

The Kiwi had made the error of applying to the Prefecture in the big smoke to erect a shed on his non-constructible land. Of course, the application was denied. CONFUSION! The French law states that you must apply for permission to erect a building that you don't need permission to erect!

"Do you understand?" said the mayor, "and NO! You CAN'T construct ANYTHING on non-constructible land!"

"But there are structures all over my non-constructible land, and they have been there for over 600 years! There are structures ALL over my twenty-five acres, including the ruins of yet another cottage, eighteen *Gariottes* (shepherds huts), and an endless amount of stone walls."

But the mayor did not falter.

"Okay, the four sides of the building on my non-constructible land are a threat to my family. Can I add roof beams to prevent these from falling down?"

This didn't seem to cause a problem. In fact, this received the mayor's support. It would save trouble should anything happen, like the building falling on a trespasser.

There are virtually no trespassing laws in rural France. People are free to wander over each other's properties, hence, the lack of fences throughout France.

Within a month, Kiwi was back in the mayor's office. He had been dobbed in to the police for building a structure on his non-constructible land. The mayor and Brenda argued his case for securing the building for safety reasons, and for the present time, the law was appeased.

Two years later and Kiwi was back in the mayor's office, having been dobbed in again to the police for adding to his roof structure to support a solar panel. Kiwi was saddened that someone had dobbed him two times now.

This seemed particularly unkind as all his neighbours were part of the hunt. There were others who forbade hunters on their property, while he openly welcomed them onto his land to shoot the *sanglier* and deer. Perhaps, Kiwi thought, there was something in the claim from World War Two, in which it was said that the French were a nation of dobbers.

He spoke of an advertising campaign in his homeland down under that hadn't gone down too well with his fellow Kiwis: "Dob in a druggy."

Kiwi went on to try and end any further dobbing in and had done extensive research for this purpose. It seemed that if people were going to dob him in, or threaten to dob him in, it was protocol that any complaint had to go before the village mayor, unless the dobber was a real nasty bit of work and would bypass the mayor and go straight to the law. The police, of course, would then have no option but to address the complaint themselves. Okay, if Kiwi got dobbed in with his next venture, he would make an endless list of ALL the illegal structures that had recently been erected on non-constructible land, including the recent animal shelters on the mayor's llama farm and dob them in officially to the police.

So now Kiwi was in the throes of constructing three huge tree-houses. He argued with himself that the structures were NOT on the land and were suspended from the trees that HE owned. He thought that when you bought land, you didn't own the mining rights, but you did own the timber rights, so his three tree-houses would be suspended from HIS trees! He had plans to create a dam and float a large raft on it, on which he would build a shed. I suppose, he thought, that this would infringe on some ancient seafaring rights.

Perhaps, thought Brenda, she was responsible for all the international friction in the village. She was recalling the stand-up blue between the Aussie and the Kiwi that terminated with the Aussie declaring, "In sports, it doesn't matter who we beat, as long as we beat New Zealand!"

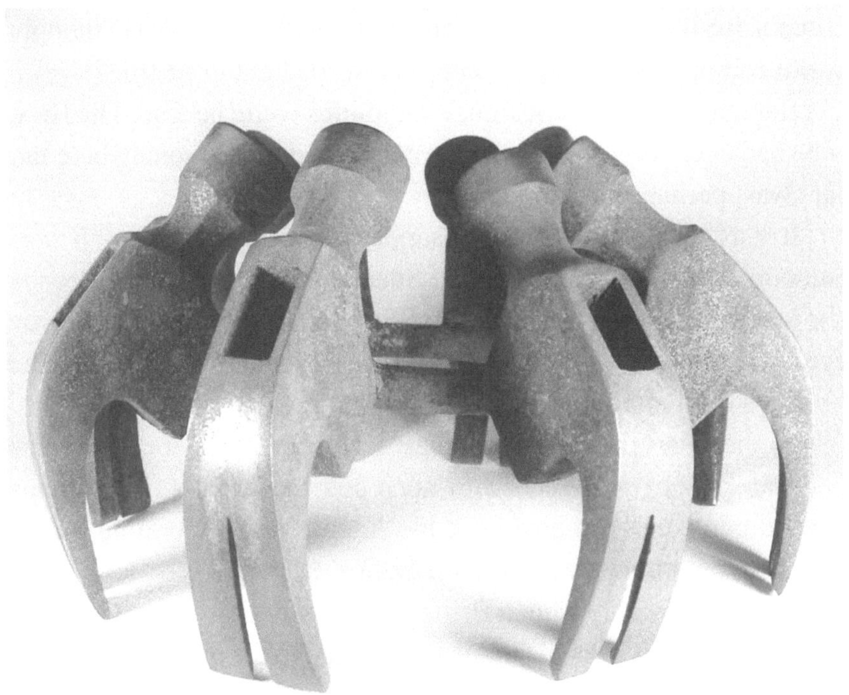

They only spoke Antipodean.

SEAMUS

According to Seamus, HE himself was responsible for every IRA bombing in the UK, Ireland, and Europe over the last six years. If he was an example of the security under which the IRA operated, then their cause was a lost one, and Brenda had said so.

Seamus's veins contained poitin brewed from Blue's potatoes, whose abundance of eyes he praised for his keen eyesight. He lived entirely on Guinness and whiskey sandwiches. He always dressed in the nation's tri-colour, which conflicted with his good taste in ties. His shoes were of the Auld Sod brand, which went soggy in the rain. Perhaps this was the reason he had moved to France.

Brenda had to be careful. It was obvious that Seamus was a compulsive liar. Still, in her last encounter with what she had thought was a compulsive liar, every word had turned out to be true.

But not one word of Seamus's ramblings *could* be true. The IRA, if he had ever been in it, would have deported him to somewhere far, far away, perhaps Tasmania.

It was true that Seamus disappeared every so often. It was rumoured that he went off to the States to raise funds, but Brenda supposed that this was all bullshit. Still, what with his steely grey eyes and extremely good looks, he was capable of charming the knickers off a nun!

In the Irish music season that occurred at the local bar, his bodhrán playing was second to none and the whistle playing was beyond compare. You could see his Adam's apple vibrating on his tremolo, something that had never been seen before.

But Brenda came from a British military background, and when she heard Seamus boasting of his uncle being in the plot to assassinate Earl Mount Crozier, she saw red.

"And I suppose that you are one of the Birmingham six, the Ellesmere seven, the Brunswick five, the Renault four, and the Peugeot 403!"

As a girl, she had moved around most of Europe, from barrack to barrack. Her father had achieved the rank of Lt. Colonel, and he was of Irish descent. Seamus accused Brenda of being a descendant from the Black and Tans, a regiment of British soldiers who occupied Eire, made up of prisoners and the scum of the British army.

Seamus strolled off on the refrain of, "Glory-O, glory-O to the bold Fenian Men!"

Brenda was sure Seamus would never forgive the words she spoke in anger.

The reason he left Belfast.

MICK

Ireland had its fair ghetto of migrants in France. Mick had been bought up in the shadows of Sampson and Goliath, the twin cranes that dominate the skyline of Belfast. At its heyday, 18,000 men worked at the shipyard. There wasn't a man in Belfast who wasn't familiar with the qualities and properties of steel, although you wouldn't believe it when you considered the fate of the Titanic! Still, it was OK when it left Belfast! Although, it was rumoured that the steel was unsuitable below zero temperatures. But all fault lay with the Brits! Didn't an Englishman sink it? And Mick said so aloud.

Mick had suffered the flash of an electric welder, which had damaged his rectum, and he had a dejected complexion cast by the echoes of the Titanic. His ears were spot welded to the side of his head. Rivets held his ample nose in place where perhaps an anchor would have been wiser. His suit had been woven from Whitworth thread, and his wristwatch was of the Vernier variety. Upon his right arm, he wore the remains of an imperial micrometer.

On his feet, he wore a lot of shoes and it was rumoured he suffered real pain, which he treated with champagne.

"Not another of your IRA smart-arsed Irish men!" spat Brenda!

"We are not all Irish Paddies!" Mick declared. "Ireland produced six presidents of the United States, forby, I am a product from the north of Ireland!"

"Then you are NOT really Irish," was Brenda's quick retort.

Mick had been trapped before by this way of thinking. Being a protestant, he was expected to be a supporter of William of Orange, and in the recent past, an advocate of Maggie Thatcher. In truth, these would all be true, but he certainly wasn't going to cow-tail to Brenda!

"What nationality are you, then?" Brenda fired at him.

"British!" he instantly replied.

A year or two ago, he had asked himself this question and had vowed that his next response would be, “Irish!”

Although loyal to the crown, he decided that he could still be proud to claim that he was Irish, but damn it, this Brenda woman had outsmarted him.

Brenda thought, “He will make me pay for that someday!”

All of a sudden, out of nowhere, the entire village was chock a block with steel workers, iron workers, and blacksmiths. It was the annual *Fete de Fer.* Mick had judged the quality of their ironwork as being equal to the passing exams expected of every schoolboy before entering the work force.

The handmade knives were doing a fair trade. What was it with the abundance of handmade knives? It was an area where French craftsmanship excelled. But why knives? Brenda knew there was a time when the French would use their own knife at the dining table, but with the number of reported stabbings, surely, the sale of knives were dwindling. In Brenda’s homeland, one could not carry a concealed knife if the blade was over three inches. Children at this exhibition were handling knives with blades of over six inches.

Around the back of the church, several blacksmiths were engaged at a crude forge, which was a fantastic sight to see. Iron ore was actually flowing from the mouth of the forge. Mick didn’t mind telling anyone who would listen that it reminded him of an essay he had read in high school.

THE ESSAY

The story is told of a tribe of West Africans. Once a year, when the moon was full, the village blacksmith and three bearers, after prayers to the sun and moon, bathing and anointed in the local river, would travel to a certain location where the wise blacksmith would make a selection of certain rocks. After prayers and thanks were given to the rocks, the three bearers carried them to a holy place with additional chanting. While the bearers rested, the blacksmith went in search of a hollowed-out tree trunk. Again, prayers and thanks were made to the gods.

The bearers were sought, who followed behind the blacksmith gathering huge amounts of firewood to be brought to the holy location. Thanks were given to the gods with more prayers. All four sat in common prayer silently for two weeks, fasting.

A storm started to blow from the west. God was thanked and prayers were made. An opening was carved on the west side of the tree stump.

The opening in the top of the stump was loaded with firewood and yet more prayers. The wood was lit, and when the fire was roaring, the rocks were introduced through the opening in the top of the log to the roaring fire below, amid continual chanting.

After two days of continually feeding the fire, the roots of the stump were finally burnt out and were replaced with solid iron. Further thanks were given to the gods. The iron was then dug up and transported back to the village. The entire village celebrated the return and praised the gods. The blacksmith then set to work fashioning tools and weapons from the iron provided by the gods.

For the tribe, there were at least thirty steps needed to produce the iron. Only six were essential. The iron ore stones, the hollow tree stump, the firewood, fire, ignition, and wind—all science. The other twenty-five steps were religion.

The tribe has long since been replaced by a mining company.

Burnt out tree trunks Fossil Beach, Cygnet.

MONSIEUR HULOT

The mayor told Brenda all about *Monsieur* Hulot, when she first came to the village. It was believed he had spent several terms in jail, though no one knew exactly what for. *Monsieur* Hulot's stained T-shirt had a copious amount, more than his standard issue, of arms. His trousers were always of the camouflage variety, which meant they were beyond description. He was surrounded by an aura of power tools and was always seen in the company of an aluminium step ladder. The top half of his body was not often seen. His legs usually protruded from underneath a dilapidated motor car. His feet had toes in numerous quantities and protruded from his toecaps, which contained enough fertilizer for the entire village.

Among the villagers, he was responsible for everything that went missing—from plants, garden implements, washing from the line, and every odd sock. In fact, it included anything that wasn't nailed down. He was the reason for a lock on every door. He was also to be blamed for interfering with the village sewerage system during the summer. Whenever the airways were polluted by radio, or any music that was too loud, *Monsieur* Hulot was blamed.

When Brenda eventually met *Monsieur* Hulot, he seemed to be a rather quiet man. His back garden, she noted, was a collection of collagenous junk. There was nothing there of real value, nothing newish.

Brenda also noticed that every time she passed Hulot's place, he seemed gainfully employed in restoring these items to their original glory.

She imagined that *Monsieur* Hulot must eventually resell these items at one of the numerous *vide greniers*.

When she mentioned this in passing to the mayor, she gathered that *Monsieur* Hulot's collection of junk was to be exchanged for another collection of junk that someone else had stolen in the next village. This was done so no one would ever be charged with any thefts. A clever ploy, thought Brenda. It wasn't until Brenda had become more fluent in her French and was beginning to use French colloquialisms that she was able to really make sense of what the mayor was trying to tell her.

"No! No! No! There is no such person as *Monsieur* Hulot. *Monsieur* Hulot is just a generalized term we French use for any unexplained incidents. Here are some examples of how we would use this expression: I can't find my spade; what happened to my pliers? Where is my screwdriver? Bloody Hulot has nicked them! I lost one sock; where's my bra? Anyone seen my false teeth? *Monsieur* Hulot has got 'em! Listen to that music blaring all over the village. *Monsieur* Hulot is to blame! Every village has its own *Monsieur* Hulot! He appears by using different names. In the neighbouring villages, there is a *Monsieur* Bois, *Monsieur* Le Blanc, and a *Monsieur* Noir!"

And here she was, Brenda, accusing *Monsieur* Hulot of all the atrocities under the sun, but during this time, he was happily going about his own business restoring his junk. She should have known that any self-respecting thief would surely select a better class of junk to steal!

Boy! Did she feel guilty! She was sure *Monsieur* Hulot knew what she'd been thinking, which would give him plenty of reason to scatter her planter boxes to the four winds!

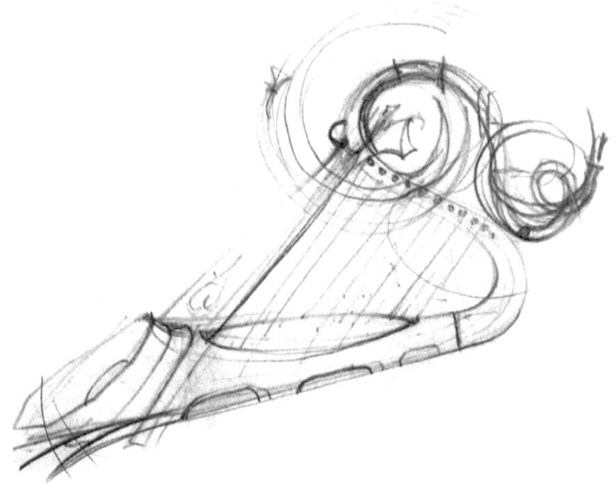

Hulots fully restored Woomera.

RICHARD TETE

Brenda had openly laughed her head off at the theories of the village conspirator. *Monsieur* Le Idiot, Richard Tete, lived in a disbanded crop circle. He was as thin as a matchstick with the wood removed, and he was surrounded by newspaper and magazine clippings that he frequently read aloud.

He wore a cape made from an Escher print, and at times, he appeared to be upside down or back to front, maybe left to right, or perhaps he was just a reflection of himself. He was the profit of doom and religious nutter all in one, and like all religious morons, Brenda noticed he was always looking forward to the day they would all be dead.

"Why do UFOs choose a fully ripened corn field and never a freshly green, sprouted one? Why are the reported incidents of UFO sightings declining, since the advent of Photoshop?" queried Brenda.

But he quickly changed the subject.

"What about the continual spraying of the upper atmosphere and all those contrails? They have removed the lead in petrol and replaced it with what? Go on! Answer that! What are we eating? Everything is modified to make sure that when we die, our bodies are polluted with synthetics that will make us easier to incinerate. Windmills? Not only do they kill our bird life, look at them, we're surrounded by dead birds!"

"I have never seen one," mused Brenda.

"Windmills also interfere with our alpha, beta, gamma, and delta rhythms. A person has only to stare at one for two minutes without blinking to induce a hypnotic trance. They can also transmit any message that the government wishes to indoctrinate us with. The prime concern of the government is to tax us almost into the level of non-existence, and it's all for their retirement funds. We subscribe to what politicians fondly call their *corruption tax*. This is a slush fund that the incoming government uses to re-grease the wheels of corruption."

Yes, Brenda had openly laughed out loud, and now she was worried. It had to be Dick Head! He was candidate *numero uno*!

Or should I wear my Escher outfit?

THE DIVINE COMEDY

When Brenda had first moved to France, they had bought a piece of farmland that was outside the village limits, which meant that it was not serviced by the town's water supply. She wanted the land for numerous reasons—to keep sheep, ducks, chickens, rabbits, and to grow vegetables. There was no water on the property, but on the advice of the mayor, she was advised to sink a well.

Monsieur Conhomme, the local Zingara, used his divining skills to divine exactly where the water was to be located. On the appointed day of his arrival, Brenda was very sceptical, because she had been reading all about water divining through her internet research. Brenda had become very devoted to the internet ever since she had heard of Schrodinger. She even had a nickname for her computer, *Schrodinger*, which reminded her of an old radio program her mother used to listen to, known as, "The Money or the Box," to which the audience would cry, "Open the box!!"

Monsieur Zingara was a professional gypsy, but the scarf around his neck was a remnant from his ancestor's profession of rat catching. He lived in constant fear of anyone with a blue form. His waistcoat showed the remains of ample empty pockets, and his trousers supported his retired family jewels. He painted his shoes. That was a tip he had learned from Spike Milligan. He thought he had all the charm of his ancestors, but in reality, he was as welcome as the Big Halt (when gypsies were forced to halt their travelling)

After spending the entire morning traversing the property and placing garden stakes at two meter intervals, the diviner came to the conclusion that there were two rivers flowing underground, and they intersected at the spot indicated by the red garden stake. He explained that his cousin owned a drilling rig, and for 2,000 euros, he could commence drilling in one week's time.

"Would water be assured?" Brenda asked.

"Well, not really," *Monsieur* Conhomme replied. "They might have to drill for an extra 1,000 euro per 20 meters."

"And then what? Can you guarantee water?"

"Well, no, we could crack a rock, and all the water could drain away."

Brenda recalled how she had read various stories on the internet that told of how ten of the world's leading water divining authorities had been invited to a gala demonstration to locate which one of ten fireman's hoses had water flowing through it. There were also thirty milk cartons on stage, and one contained a bar of gold. The challenge was for each contestant to use their ten chances at selecting which hose had water flowing through it and which milk carton contained the bar of gold. Each contestant was given three attempts, with a proviso that if he or she got one right out of the three, then this would be attributed to luck.

Even with the advantage of luck, not one of the contestants succeeded. They all pleaded that dowsing NEVER works in the presence of a sceptic!

Yes, Brenda thought, she was a sceptic, and the mayor's friend was just another conman as his name suggested. She had no hesitation of telling him so. She said that the entire underground world was honeycombed with rivers flowing everywhere, and it was obvious by the number of wells on the surrounding properties that eventually water would seep into it. All someone had to do was sink a hole anywhere in the area to make this happen.

Another suspect for Brenda's list.

Zingaras brothers water drilling rig.

ENTREPRENEUR

Then there was that Parisienne, fair weather invader who was forever introducing novel and irrelevant ways, to the *Patrimoine* for raising funds, *Mademoiselle* Entrepreneur. Her latest idea was ridiculous.

"You CAN'T do that to the BLUE'S!" Brenda was absolutely adamant.

"It is one thing to present classical music, even opera highlights in the church but no I can't support you putting on a concert of the Blues, it's WRONG, WRONG, WRONG! Blues comes from the sleazy, smokey back streets of music. It is sad, its passionate, it's Bluesy! Played and sung by people with souls that cry, drowned in alcohol and drugs. You can't dress it up, repackage it and play it on a Steinway and have it sung by a squeaky clean, bakewell tart, ship shaped Bristol fashioned, Victoria sponge, Mormon choired Christian grinning from ear to ear!

The audience who attend concerts that are performed in churches are supposedly respectable or would like to present themselves as respectable!Look at the way they dress up!"

Brenda was warming up now. "They are dressed as if they are going to church, which they are and they will applaud appropriately. No! It is all WRONG! Where's the smoke, where's the alcohol, where's the sex, where are the drugs? Where are the BLUES?" (*All forbidden by the church*)

Wow! Did Brenda let fly! But then Blues was her favorite music only because she THOUGHT that she could sing it. After all it didn't demand perfection, just absolute conviction and absolute soul! And the priest? Will this be the same priest that wouldn't allow the Merry Widow Waltz to be among last years opera highlights?

At its height the foot and mouth scare in England became part of the English psyche and it certainly never failed Brenda. She was permanently affected, yes, every time she opened her mouth she put her foot in it! Revenge would be sought over that altercation, but Brenda was proud of these issues, wasn't she equally in her rights to let people know just how SHE felt?

Blues harp ???

THE MARKET

As Brenda wandered through the weekly market on her way to the cafe, she thought to herself that the French had a strange relationship with their animals. All the flesh and meat on display still had their heads attached. She thought this must be due to a law that assured customers that the meat was as it was claimed to be. But if so, why wasn't there a horse's head on the stalls that sold horse meat? She supposed that the fowls could be easily confused, because the variety was huge. Customers had their choice of quality, guinea fowl, *pintade*, duck, or goose.

She learned from the reissue of old magazines that all the four-legged animals, which included goats, pigs, dogs, and sheep were considered beasts of burden. Chickens and geese were kept on a lease. The English had a fondness for their dogs, and they even allowed them into their pubs. In certain areas of Great Britain, farmers actually had portraits of their sheep in place of their spouse.

These days, it was unsafe to wander along the canals in England. Dog shit was spread the entire length of the towpath. To slip and drown in the cut would make you the latest victim. Watching Brits walking along the towpath is like watching a ballet of sorts, to see their accomplished movements trying to avoid the heaped-up turds. The walk among Bargees was referred to as the dog-poo shuffle. When it came to domesticated pets, the French and English were as bad as each other, pondered Brenda.

Time for an aperitif, she thought to herself as she opened the door to the crowded Cafe Merde. *Monsieur* Hulot and Mick where chatting at the bar.

"Whats that rubbish your drinking?" asked Mick "looks like a drop of the hard stuff!"

Monsieur Hulot was sitting at the bar on the outside of a forgotten, warm Guinness.

"You should know, its the life blood of your native sod!" Hulot scowled.

"That stuffs rubbish, thats not Guinness!"

"Of course it is, it says so on the can!"

"Just because it sounds like a duck, looks like a duck, doesn't mean to say it is a duck. It could be the Mayor dressed up like a duck saying quack, quack, quack!"

"What?" enquired Hulot "I am drinking a duck?!"

"No! thats just an expression I could have said a cow,"

"You mean its milk!"

"No forget it! I want out!" But Mick continued "Guinness have spent millions trying to export real stout from Ireland. The stuff just doesn't travel, just like you Frogs! They've dressed it up, added, subtracted and multiplied it and ended up with that stuff there" pointing at Hulots glass "it looks like stout, it smells like stout, but is it stout? The manufacturers have spent millions destroying the origins of the personal Guinness and as I said the original thing is like you, it doesn't travel"

"What do you mean I don't travel?"

"I have never met a Frenchmen in my life before I came to live in France. In fact the last Frenchman to visit England arrived on the beach and was hung as a spy" Mick burst into song-

He's got long legs, a great long tale,
He's covered all in hair
We thought he was a spy
So we hanged him in the square.
(From the Hartlepool Monkey by Alan Wilkinson)

"I've never met one in Ireland, Wal and Bluey reckon they have never met one in Oz. I reckon those French Canadians got lost with the rest of the Eskimos who made it over the land bridge from Asia to Canada or was that from the North Island of New Zealand to

Tanzania or Tasmania? Bet those guys forgot they were French!" His knowledge of geography was bordering on the shy to the awkward.

"The only outside influence you guys get is from those lanky, salted licorice eating, tulip smoking, dyke walkers! When they holiday here there is no interrelating with them, they have bought everything with them, all their food, meat, veggies, bread, they are as mean as Scrooge!"

"So that is what meant by going Dutch?"

But there was no stopping Mick "No! You guys holiday in your own country, I am surprised that you allow your ducks to migrate! None of you get out of the place! I am amazed that you're even indulging in that excuse for Guinness, next you'll be telling me that you have just eaten a pack of salt and vinegar chips !"

"What on earth are you raving about?!" Cried Hulot.

But it was no good, Mick was on his hobby horse. "Look, I'll spell it out for you! To an Irishman Guinness has always been a personal brew. For a start, the brewers supply stout to any given bar. The individual barman in Ireland has been pulling individual pints from four individual barrels. For example, number one barrel could have just been freshly tapped, number two barrel might be almost empty, number three might be a third full, number four, half empty. The particular barman will pull your pint knowing exactly how much is in each barrel at all times. He will individually blend your pint from all four of the barrels, keeping an eye on the continual change of level in each barrel and changing the blend accordingly."

"Sounds like a disaster for a nightmare!" chipped in Brenda, who had been listening to every word these two were saying. To add to her confusion she couldn't understand how these two got through such a complicated conversation, as *Monsieur* Hulot could not understand a word of English and Mick was illiterate in all languages.

"What I suggest you do" said Mick "is to broaden your mind, get out of France, for your next holidays, go to Ireland, visit Liams bar in Magherafelt and ask Aiden the barman for one of Micks stouts. Don't rush him, give him your order, and grab a seat. He'll ring his bell when it is prepared, black gold! You can tell it is the real stuff, every mouthful leaves its signature around the glass, I might see you there!" He wandered off in a Guinness cloud of dreams and memories.

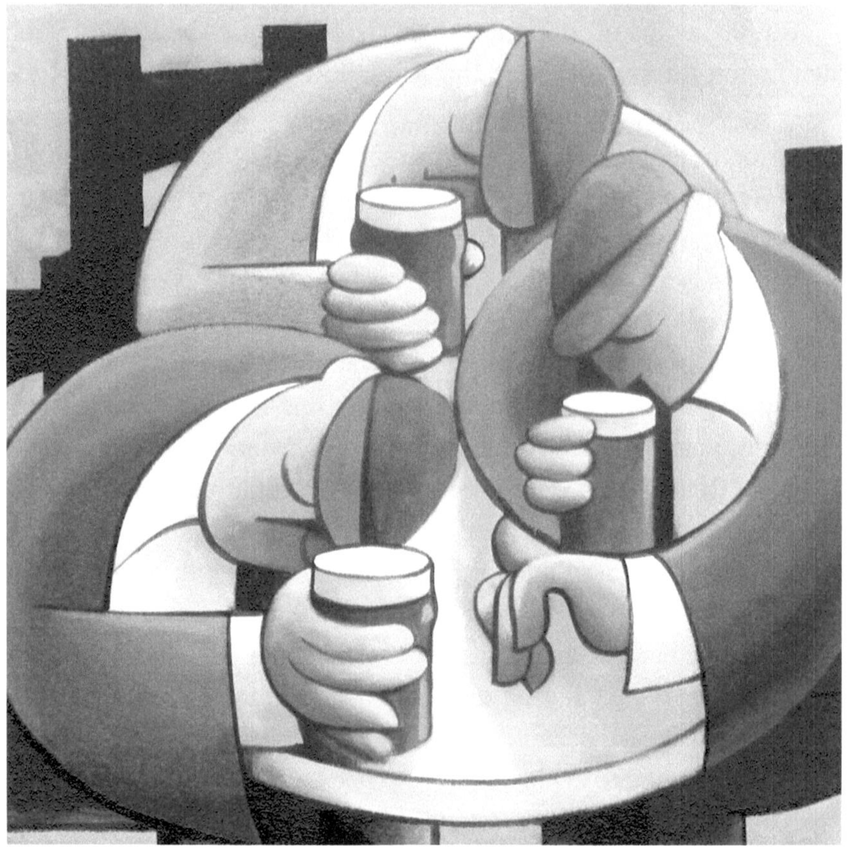

The personal effects of Guinness.

CAFE MERDE

There had been plans to turn the local restaurant café into a really posh eating place, and this is what had initially lured Wally, Bluey's mate, into bidding for the position of chef. The exciting culinary experiences at home had led to an understanding that being a chef in France would be his Eldorado, his Shangri-La, his Woolloomooloo of cuisine.

The very thought of Woolloomooloo started his culinary appendages throbbing and he could barely contain himself as he relived his salivated moments in the dock area of Bloodykingscross (one word). That location was where he had regularly and patiently encountered the amazing delights of Pete's Pie Stall!

Ahh! A pie floater!

A bowl of steamy hot marrow fat peas, on which floated a National Meat Pie, or was it Four and Twenty? Surely, it didn't have blackbirds baked in it, right? All topped with a piquant endorsement of tomato ketchup. The thought of it brought tinnies to his eyes!

But here he was in the shaded side of the village square, along with the wall flowers and the redundant sundial, (thank goodness the bus had run into the fountain as that saturated monstrosity had dampened his amorous attitude) up to his ears in *foie gras* and a hundred varieties of duck.

He had tried in vain to introduce culinary spices into the lives of these French frog-eating peasants. Bugger it! He was off home to Oz, after he stopped spending his money on wine, women, and song and wasting the rest.

Wal was convinced that the French were born with taste bud receptors only for duck!

The conclusion or upshot of all this was that Bluey and he were not only soul mates in sport and lager, but there was some truth in what Brenda had claimed. The pair of them had food Asperger's and compulsive eating disorders.

Aussies were like their milk—homogenized. They had done for food what the Irish had done for music.

"Christ!" said Wal. "There isn't a vibrato of music that doesn't have an Irish bar in it!"

He's right, thought Brenda. Bar is the word!

"And where would American music be without Mick's semi-quavers? Or the Fenians' rhythm? Weren't they the ones who taught those folks in Harlem how to play the spoons and hambone? Where would their sense of rhythm be, without their jigs and reels? What about Chandos singing? Without that, American shape notes would be redundant!"

"Rock and roll would be lost without all that gyrating and swinging of the hips!" said Kiwi.

Kiwi had just joined the discussion.

"Piss off!" said Bluey. "Wal and me are talking about food. I was telling how Aussies had travelled back to their ancestral homes to teach these mongrels how to cook their own awful food."

"Just like us Brits did in England!" added Brenda. "Our Indian curries leave the Indian food that you get over in India to shame! Not only is the meat superior, but the herbs and spices come directly from India." (Something in that didn't ring true, she thought.)

"Yeah," said Bluey. "You have just gotta watch any food show on TV, regardless if it's Italian, French, Spanish, Mexican, or Indian. You will definitely see what us Aussies have done for food!"

Poor Wal! He'd tried so hard, but he'd given up! The criteria for a restaurant succeeding in France included tradition and loyalty; quality never entered the equation. Price was the priority.

Brenda butted in, "Sure, everything is about pricing!" she exclaimed.

"What's your beef?" demanded Wally. "Food is our priority, and it depends on quality! Consider your *Entrecote* steak. Can you think of any other way of buggering up so many cuts of steak in one slice? And what about *faux* steak? What do they mean that it's the wrong steak? The only thing that's wrong with it is that it was put into the hands of a French butcher! And my goodness! The spuds! You can't tell the difference between a turnip and any variety of their waxy, watery, potatoes!"

"No!" said Mick. "We had a great spud the other day. Bintjes, I've been told."

"Dutch!" blurted Brenda.

Mick had joined the farce, and everyone thought that he would be the authority on spuds.

"Well, they are really as good as Blues back home."

He really didn't mean it (He had the same opinion of Blues music), but he was tired of these two behaving like two whinging Aussie Poms (which they weren't).

Suddenly a hush came over the bar and in walked a complete stranger to everyone.

The stranger wore a tired expression over his entire outfit. The exotic expressions on his face he had inherited from his ancestors, who had escaped the guillotine, were expanding daily. If he was in England it would be said that he dressed like a squire, except for his cravat which unfurled from every crevice. His shoes were of the articulated choice which he spoilt by wearing odd socks, of which he owned a similar pair at home. He had an authoritative air about him, probably achieved by the motor bike helmet that he carried. His entire appearance was focused on his gold rimmed glasses which were currently residing in his breast pocket.

He sat down to read his newspaper, but a more astute observer would have noticed that he was checking each patron over the top of it. The accordion checkered bar had quietened the moment he had entered. There was a pause of pregnancy in the air until Mick went on with his rave.

"I suppose you reckon they are as good as your Maris Piper or King Edwards?" But Bluey had changed the subject.

"What about those snails? I have never seen a Frenchman eat them!"

"Their mussels look great," said Brenda.

"Those are Blue Lips from New Zealand!" Kiwi exclaimed.

"And what's more," he went on to say, "they have discovered at Stonehenge that the Brits were devouring those frog legs three thousand years before the French!"

"Did someone call me?" It was Maris, the music teacher.

"No!" everyone declared in harmony, in one accord.

"Surely, I heard my name?"

"Ahh," said Brenda. "They were talking about MARIS PIPER POTATOES!"

"Didn't he play the Uillean pipes?" inquired Mick.

"Will the lot of you buzz off? Bluey and I are trying to have a barney about food!" said Wal.

All this, and they hadn't even started on the bread!

Brenda knew this was a sore point, because the pair of Aussies had gotten into trouble with the local *boulangerie*. "You buy the stuff at eight in the morning, and by the time you get it home, it's stale!" they had declared.

Brenda exclaimed, "French bread never passed the Bovril test with me!"

Her way of judging the size of the holes in a sandwich was to spread her Bovril and see if it dripped down her arm before it reached her adequate mouth.

But it was too late! Everyone had knocked off arguing to stop for lunch, which Wal had prepared earlier. Soup was the watery remains from the pressure cooker and a stock cube that the three veggies had been cooked in, all together. A choice of gizzards in lettuce, gizzards in lettuce, or gizzards in lettuce! The main course was duck cooked in three ways, canard, on its own, or barely dead! Surprise! The meal ended with *creme brulee* (English custard and French burnt sugar).

One hundred and fifty-six varieties of cheese; so much effort, and they never got it right!

"Isn't that the guy from the bar?" whispered Wal

"It is, he is looking over here!"

"Watch it! He's getting up!"

"Whose he?" said Maris

"SHHHHHH! I think he's coming over here...... his is!!!....."

They had all moved from the bar and were now sitting in the pseudo Charles De Gaul airport style, restaurant section, of the limpid building.

They had just finished their meal and were dealing with the remains of the red wine.

"Looks like he is heading our way!" said Kiwi.

"Watch it!" said Mick "I think he's going to join us!"

"May I interrupt?" He spoke in fluent English as only a Frenchman can. "I couldn't help over hearing what you gents were talking about"

With an air of graceful servility he went on "Everyone is entitled to their opinion, and of course in many instances you are probably right, but hey guys! You are going a bit far when you start to rubbish our bread!" He paused for a cultured break to let his words sink in. He sat down in Maris's seat. She was off to the loo, she would be gone for hours as the washroom had an embellished resonation that sympathized with anyone singing in E flat!

"Let them drink the remains of that lazy red, I'm going to break the soprano barrier today!" Maris was in her dream world!

"You know just because Napoleon was defeated at the battle of Waterloo it doesn't mean to say that he got it wrong!" the stranger continued.

"Thats smart" thought Wal "just cos you lose an argument, even a war, doesn't mean to say you're wrong! Kiwi's always winning our arguments but I know the sheep shagging mongrels' wrong ALL the time!" While Wal was still having his rightful thoughts, the stranger went on, "We are still using his legal system..He was the first general in battle to lighten the weight of his metal standards by having them cast in aluminum. The ambulance on the battle field? That was his idea! Then there is that rubbish that you Brits are still spreading on, dare I say it, bread, or should I say sliced preservatives? I am talking about margarine ! The Brits misunderstood that it was only to be used by the troops in the field as the butter was always going rancid. Now the Brits have manufactured the stuff by the millennium and spread it all over the entire nation, which is probably a good idea. (He had forgotten that he was an aristocratic illuminated example of WOW!) Napoleon had all those avenues of plane trees planted along the main routes so that his troops could march in the shade!"

"Rubbish!" mumbled Kiwi "they would have been to small to give much shade!"

But this Aristocrat drowned his mumbles "I felt I had to interrupt when you came to criticizing our bread! I have been observing your table manners and your eating etiquette and it became obvious that you just don't get it! With a capital 'I'! You gentlemen are groomed to the British use of the knife and fork! To us French, bread is not only a food but an additional eating tool, its used almost like a fork but not quite, it is for pushing against, it is to stop you chasing peas around the room! Our bread is ideal, the crust is strong and lasts the duration of the meal, the inner is to soak and mop up the gravy and juices. It has not been baked for a long duration, what is left after the meal is fed to the animals or soaked in tomorrows soup. A fresh batch is baked for the evening meal. It is NOT meant to last, consequently no preservatives are needed, like that rubbish at the supermarket!"

"Yer in MY seat!" Maris had returned.

" Whose hit a bum note?" thought Bluey.

"Terribly sorry, pardon." the stranger replied in ten different polygloted languages. In French style he hadn't introduced himself but made his indifferent departure with the air of an allured dignitary. He added "I live beyond the next village, beyond the pale and over the panorama. Perhaps I could invite you all to dine with me whenever you are in my direction. Our local restaurant does a very fine *gezzier* salad, *foie gras*, *canard de canard*, *creme brulee*, all to be washed down with, of course, our fine Red!" He turned around and came back "You know us French didn't leave our caves to become a nation of binge drinkers!"

The strangers name was Sebastian Delacroix, but he wasn't going to tell that to any of this lot!

"Well! He certainly put you in your place!" said Maris.

"What do you mean? You were there too!"

"No I wasn't! I was singing in the loo!"

Brenda spoke up "I'm surprised he didn't mention that the French meal has gained recognition by the world heritage listing."

"I've heard that" said Wal, the chef "that wasn't for the food but for the way the French eat, how they sit down together for their family meals, how wine is always present at every meal, it is a complete family occasion!"

"What about Bovril?" declared Brenda

"I know this one!" said Wal "It was Napoleon who invented that."

"I got a wedge of Stilton that I ordered on the web along with Melton Mowbray pies and some sausage rolls, ten loaves of real bread, four jars of Heinz vegetable spread, a pound of dolly mixtures, and a dozen bhaji's," Brenda declared too loudly. Had the stranger heard her?

The cafe had been crowded that day others too would have heard that last outburst!

Theres not much room in here for that sort of thing.

ENCORE BRENDA

For the second time, Brenda stormed into the mayor's chambers. This time, she was breathing fire! On her way down to his office that morning, she had recalled an old farming story from Ireland that her grandfather had told her about two neighbouring farmers who were always at loggerheads with each other.

One farmer had commenced his ploughing, when he hit a rock with his newly sharpened ploughshare and broke the tip off. He went to get his spare, only to remember that it had been left at the village blacksmith for repair over a year ago.

His neighbour and traditional enemy (for reasons long forgotten, but which he knew had to do with something that Brian Boru had done to Finn McCool) was Farmer Grump. Farmer Grump, in his goody-two-shoes fashion, would not only have a freshly sharpened ploughshare, but the smart ass would have two or three spares. Surely, he would loan him one of his spares?

As he journeyed along the short distance to his neighbour's farm, he turned over the thought in his mind all the reasons that his neighbour would give him for not loaning him his ploughshare.

"Sure, didn't your great, great, grandfather never return the scythe he borrowed, and wasn't the handle broken on the spade your father borrowed? If I loaned you a new point for your plough, you would just return it all rusty!"

All this negativity was churning in his gut, and his hopes were sinking further down in his boots. He hesitated when he reached Grumps' doorstep. He turned to go, but with a final effort, he knocked feebly on the door. All was silent, but then with all of the courage of his ancestors, he banged furiously on the door. The door was finally opened by Farmer Grump.

“You can stick your ploughshare straight up your arse! I wouldn’t borrow it if it was the last ploughshare on earth! So there!” he fumed, before turning to plod his way wearily homeward.

Brenda thought she was behaving just like that farmer.

She gathered her thoughts, then in a fire-breathing monologue, she declared in a fury what had happened to her planter boxes. She demanded satisfaction, revenge, and vengeance in one foul sweep.

It took the mayor an eternity to calm Brenda down so that he could make sense of her outburst.

“Oh, that!” murmured the mayor. “I was hoping...hmmm…that it had...all...blown away.”

“WHAT was that?” said Brenda, furiously.

“Oh, that!” repeated the mayor. “I was hoping that would be all cleared up by the time I returned from Scotland.”

“What do you mean?” asked Brenda, suspicion edging her voice.

Surely she’d never offended the mayor?

“Mr. Sebastien Delacroix, who lives on the extreme edges of the community, on a hill beyond a hill, beyond a hill, well, he lives there on a large property behind not only an extremely high electrified fence, but a second stone wall, as well. There is only one way in and out of the property. Security is controlled by every known electronic device and includes a double layer of gates.

Well, he had some animals that were supposed to be delivered to his property, but the delivery van had an accident negotiating one of the bends through the village. One of the crates fell off the truck and smashed open. It contained a family of baboons. The baboons ran amuck in the village, eventually arriving at your planter boxes, which they stripped of flowers and finally overturned all of them! They were probably attracted by the smell of fresh goat manure that was used. Mr. Delacroix reported to me what had happened, but by the time he got his act together, the baboons had disappeared into the surrounding hills. I thought all this would have been cleared up, because he had promised to make instant restitution, especially as four raccoons had escaped from his menagerie two years ago and are now breeding in the wild! Anyhow, Brenda, I hope that none of this has caused you too much concern, but as we say in France, *C’est La Vie*!”

The ship of Fools.

www.ingramcontent.com/pod-product-compliance
Ingram Content Group UK Ltd.
Pitfield, Milton Keynes, MK11 3LW, UK
UKHW041925190726
13854UKWH00003B/1458

9 781483 408965